Curbside Pickup

ISBN #978-0-557-04762-8

Library of Congress Cataloging-in-Publication Data available.

Vanity Pressed by Dead Uncle Ivan

First Edition

Design & Artwork by Chris Rubino

info@curbsidepickup.net | www.curbsidepickup.net

Curbside Pickup

• • •

D Edward Ennis

working relationship

it was shortly after George
Ding caught me fucking his
wife that i started
calling him ShortStack and
PennyRoll he said it made
him uncomfortable i felt
it brought us closer
together how we'd banter
back and forth casual in
the early morning air as
we hung off the end of the
garbage truck hopping off
in irregular intervals to
pile more filth and unwant into
the belly of that beast she was
a special woman George Ding's
wife with her long gold hair
her permanent black eye and
a smile like you read about

Pete's dream

passing a stone had been easier
than he'd anticipated instantly awash
in intense depression and
anxiety Pete began to fear fried
clams and all forms
of talk radio finding solace
the only way he knew Pete over-
indulged in grain alcohol cigar-
illos big band jazz and swimsuit
catalogs a fixture at the local
beaches all along the South Shore that
Summer Pete's mental health
rapidly diminished as his knowledge of the
tankini and other two-pieces increased
walking the shoreline Pete kicked at the
smooth beach stones while harboring
a secret desire to pass each one

in the event

in late afternoon rainstorms
during the Summer you should be
barefoot if possible with a
friend who is likewise barefoot you
should endure its entirety despite
the fact that you continue
to pass by your house on the corner
you should make as many bold meteor-
ological claims as you can muster
regardless of their potential invalidity if
the storm picks up in intensity your
t-shirt should be removed and
tied around your head as if
you are Lawrence of Arabia when the
storm subsides you should remain
in your rain soaked shorts for the
remainder of the evening if
you own a guitar it should be
played on the porch late into
the night

over at the fairgrounds

knee deep in Saturday's throbbing
rebuttal to Friday night's alcohol
poisoning at the Marshfield Fairgrounds
these jerking movements one then
another and all the loose change
and mints dangling from each
stoically bent appendage you've
gone off and spelt 'sorry' in the
sand with grape soda and catsup while
i'm stuck picnicking in the back of
my mind watermelon soaked resentment
shoots from my mouth and into
the checkered napkin you've
tuct into the front of your holiday
shirt as i blurt out 'you are a
horror Kim, truly, despite your trust
fund and all your very homosexual friends'

future plans

Susan whisks herself from room to room
and kitchen the ice bucket cheese dome
and other wedding gifts nostalgic
and dated carefully positioned throughout
and then the doorbell all the invitations folded
in shirt pockets or left on dashboards out front
Mark in his new brown loafers hovers around
the stereo a Virgo hiding behind
the vaguely contemporary playlist until all
guests have shuffled off into
the late Summer midnight save
for professor Figgins and his
dimwitted and voluptuous dinner
date Janet searching for her shoes in
the half bath chances are
they'll not entertain again until
the new year perhaps as late as
Spring for their social standing always
falters alongside Mark's election year
paranoia and seasonal hermitic devotion

tradition

Bruce had packed his suitcase
the night before everything
neatly sectioned off by the
cardboard dividers he'd
inserted long ago and
left it in the foyer
next to the front door the
annual trip to York Beach has
been the highlight of Bruce's
year for the last 37 years so
much so that the anticipation alone
was itself intensely pleasurable
as he sat in the family van parked
out front and meticulously packed
since 6:30 that morning Bruce
honked the horn for Amy and the
boys anxious to beat the traffic
settle into the rented cottage and eat
his first bubble gum ice cream
cone before the sun set

portion control

back in the small town of his childhood
Carl now discovered himself full circle
and after some many odd years of living in
the city he found himself relearning the importance
of appearances just being white was no longer enough
he now had to be careful not to linger on his way past
the neighborhood bus stops in the mornings or outside of
the church centers in the evenings and most importantly
to never find himself with a suspicious amount of
popsicles in the grocery store check out

egg rolls

'maybe the chicken and
the string beans'd be
nice the beans are in
season' she says in
rounded words muffled by
the thick pink fingers of
the hand she rests her
chins on words which go un-
acknowledged by the young
couple seated across the
table she isn't looking at
the menu she says it because
she has nothing better to say
they're the only other people
in the Shing Yee Restaurant at
4:45 on a sunny Sunday Summer
afternoon i shift my attention
to the empty bottle in front of
the empty chair in front of me and
well at least she's got someone to
say really uninteresting things to
i don't even like egg rolls i
didn't want to look like a slob
ordering just a beer

the release

her form was sound and the
release was solid but as soon
as the ball made contact with
the lawn it took a sharp right
and as it rolled to a slow
stop the pallino lay un-
touched a good 7 yards
away and with that one bad
bounce the Neighborhoods of
Stanley Annual Backyard Bocce
Tournament was ended the trophy
cooler rattling with bottled beer
and hard lemonade would go
to the Pierces this year and with
that one bad bounce Kathleen knew
she would not have to endure another
long Winter listening to Mike's tire-
some speeches on destiny and dynasty

safe and sorry

there was a solar eclipse that day
they taught us in school to not
look directly at it we made
pinhole viewers out of our dads'
shoe boxes it was also dental
hygiene day we chomped on red
pills that turned our plaque
pink and we watched a film strip
about a crocodile and a bird then
we took home tooth brushes and
tiny tubes of Crest Steve and i
spent the rest of the day in
Sheldon's Vacant Lot catching
tadpoles he'd squeeze them I'd
fill them up with toothpaste
a few dozen floated in a minty
film at the top of the stagnant
hole full of rain water and as
evening came guilt overtook us
and we ran home for dinner

job well done

exhausted through and through
after following all the
Swedish Pop bands on the
global Summer festival
circuit Chuck entered
his apartment to
find that Natalie had
taken excellent care of
his plants and left neat
piles of his mail categorized
and alphabetized on his
kitchen counter peeking
in his fridge expecting a
combination of expired dairy
items and rotted vegetables
he found that she'd restocked it
he now realized that the
Helsinki-Malmi Airport paper-
weight was not going to be an
adequate thank you and wondered
if instead he should finally invite
Natalie up for sex

in her defense

back in the days of
basketball camp at the
local community college
they'd have 5 gallon coolers
full of the stuff generic
powder fruit punch mix
they called it bug juice
and bug juice is exactly what
Mrs. Mills was offering
Jeffrey on this warm Autumn
afternoon originally volunteering
to take the old woman's trash
to the curb on Thursday mornings
Jeffrey unwittingly discovered himself
employed as a landscaping
handyman far below the minimum
wage it was easy enough work
save the extra care required
to avoid the various pots
and tin cans she'd
strung about the yard to
alert her to the presence of
the habitual Peeping Toms that
frequented her trees

the south side of town

i've this time seen the neighbors carry underbrush
to the curb out front and i have this time seen cinder
blocks thrown from the wrought iron fire escapes
i've this time not seen discarded umbrellas on the
MDC walk and i have this time not ever seen children
fleeing from large cardboard boxes by the train tracks
i'm saying i've seen things in the neighborhood and
i'm saying i'ven't seen things in the neighborhood
i can walk down any street i want any time i want

Norm's long awaited morning

(or 46 years of marriage)

Norm came down the stairs
quieter than he had the previous
morning enough chill on the floor to
justify the brown corduroy slippers
Lois caught a glimpse of his feet when
she heard him in the doorway not
surprised at all that Norm had pulled
the ragged old things out of the
trash after last Spring's cleaning
and best not to acknowledge it
she thought rolling the sausages
across the pan with a popping sizzle
as that would certainly make his day

irreplaceable

retracing my walk home from
Julio's been searching for my silver
Timex since waking on a lawn of
dead leaves sometime near dawn
and now've got 2 vanilla Cokes
Raisinettes and little else in
my belly and you i should've left you
in bed Scotty yelling obscenities
at the birds and squirrels while shaking
your Expos hat at the few passing cars
and turning the corner past
Brick's Washateria the sun stings
our eyes and we squat beneath
an awning sharing my last bent
cigarette not even all that certain
i ever owned a watch like that

public viewing

Nancy'd been plagued with
confidence issues ever since
the Recital Incident of
'82 she thought she'd bottomed
out after coming home from a
Hampton Beach long weekend
with a Sylvester & Tweety tattoo
on the back of her right shoulder
and yet here she was a dozen years
later working at the public
library returning books to their
shelves with her hair up in
a bun her tight blouse short
skirt and complete lack of
underwear

continuing

it was late in the Fall season and for all intents
and purposes Wayne had managed to alienate himself
from the bulk of the adult education volleyballers
at the high school it wasn't so much his
many misplays at the net or even his habit of
muttering 'whore' whenever he failed to return a
serve it was very simply his lack of wrist-
bands and his tendency to sweat profusely from
the elbow on down just last Thursday Mary had to be
assisted off the court after upending in a pool
of his perspiration shortly after a late match rotation

cotton waist

the challenge now and for the
foreseeable future includes a
finely tuned blender a series
of highly skilled Pictionary games
and the bland ramblings of your
tax attorney-middle management-
savings & loan type neighbors now
listen Roger you can panic could
falter and i'd understand believe
me but you must stick out
your chest Roger must muster some
bravado a touch of gusto and
strongarm your way straight through
this relentless run of Family Game
Nights and know this my thoughts
will be with you always

the goby

it started raining last week for the first time
since Ernest moved into the 2nd floor apartment
across from the park one continuous puddle covers
all three blue basketball courts if and
when he's been drinking he starts thinking he's living
across from the aquarium again even took to
naming the empty Coke cans and/or Frito Lay bags after
some of the more popular tropical fish
is the Trojan wrapper the banded goby
or the bar goby

time off

it was purchased seven months ago
and it is just now that Henry
is able to sit back now that the
mowing is over the clapboards patched
and painted leaves raked and
hauled off it is now that Henry is able to
sit back in his study with the blinds
raised looking out across his
lawn through the bare trees
at the church steeple in the
waning afternoon light and empty
his tumbler of scotch in quiet
anticipation of Winter's first snowfall

Scotty's big American romance

tractor trailers are no longer
romantic Scotty not tractor trailers not
trainyards not toy soldiers nobody
dreams of these things anymore i know
you wince with fond remembrance of
heavy die cast metal toys from
your youth i dropt marbles from
your second story window imagining
the splatter of cat eyes nobody can
turn a trainyard into anything but
a trainyard a soldier a soldier you
see but it pains you Scotty as it
pains me too

Gary accepts leadership of the lodge

it was a pregnant pause for certain one
with beads of sweat and a shivering
of anticipation one that burst into a bevy
of applause and glasses raised up to
toast words that slipped off whiskied
tongues and stumbled across gin soaked
lips like so many sullied salutations be-
fore but this this was Gary's night and he wasn't
about to let that bitch Tina ruin it

this Sunday's charity brunch

sorry Larry you've caught
me in the bath again given
much consideration to the
surgery just can't miss out
on the overtime shifts yes
i've seen your missing calico
posters all across town
only time will tell and/or
heal all wounds come to
think of it you're sure to be
a smash at this Sunday's charity
brunch with your Taste Of
Americana picture postcard
display and your slightly
affected but altogether
convincing Walt Whitman
readings

alliances

she was getting around much
easier but still Mary decided to
sit out the holiday party at her
husband's beloved French American Club
she'd never cared for the lodge its dank
yellow walls and yellower ceiling
tiles or the furniture that
predated the club itself not antique
or classic just old and tired much
like the bunch who drinks there
every night save Monday most importantly
Mary really didn't see the point at all
boudin blanc at Christmastime the
Bastille Day Celebrations instead of
the 4th his insistence on fresh baguettes
at every dinner party it could've made
sense it would've made sense if
either Gary or herself were even
the slightest bit French

snow day

it was Friday and there
was no work me and
Scotty sat at the bar
eating chili and chips
drinking the better part
of five hours the snow
rapidly fell as predicted
the few other customers sat
quietly intently
waiting out the storm
the snow was up to our
knees when we stepped
outside stopping
intermittently to help
push cars from their spots
along the street we
made our way to the
packy and leaving the store
Scotty slipped and found
himself lying on his back
making something like a
snow angel as he scrambled
to collect his scattered Schlitz
Tall Boys from beneath the bed
of snow

coming soon

after confirming that the market was
down for the third straight day
Victor removed the ice pack from
his shoulder and walked down to
the living room to see if his
boots had dried the fire still
burned strong but the boots were
cold and damp inside he laced
them up in the garage and stepped
out into what were to be the last
falling flakes of this storm chipping
the ice from the stairs Victor
imagined the relief that his retirement
would bring this coming Spring the
Winters in South Carolina maybe Georgia
and visits from the grandchildren Victor
smiled as he broke loose the last stubborn
patches of ice from the front walk
hoping he'd never need do it again

arrangements

intimate sleeping arrangements had
long troubled George including not one
but several unbearably awkward nights at
Camp Kiwanee in the hot Summers of
his youth George was unsure of what
prompted this memory as he stared
at the ash gray bricks lining the back
of the fireplace he wanted the fire to
die out so he could head to bed and
at the same time he was enjoying the
memory of those long Summer nights
spent listening to the crickets the frogs
the breathing and light snores of his
bunkmates desperately hoping one might
wake and ask him to slip out
behind the boat house and as the fire
slowly died out George knew it was
time to get some sleep and knew his
wife was never coming back and wondered
if it was too late for him

response time

a tremendous response was
underway as the news rippled
from house to house person
to person down both sides
of the icy street and clear
across town Margaret's
first bout of tears had
yet to dry nor had Victor
yet reached the morgue before
the first casserole made its way
up the front walk

getting away

up on blocks with its
top down it didn't
matter to Katie that
the old Thunderbird hadn't
moved an inch in her lifetime
she'd sit with her dolls
her friends or herself
driving into an imagined
horizon somewhere beyond
the unpainted back of
the garage door despite
this car being relegated to
plaything Katie had not one
single thing to hold on to
except for the hope that it
could maybe someday bring
her far far away

the things you don't forget

we were nine when Aubrey
told me he didn't like music
i've never forgotten
that i heard he is working
on a calculus doctorate
down in Tampa his
sister recognized me
at the bar i'm much heavier
now and she is much older
there was once a time
when she'd stand in the
corner and pull her dress
up for no real reason at all
not anymore though

fishing

somewhere between the final frost
and the first flower Leo was
caught finding it harder every
morning to determine what to
wear today he'd come down to
the diner in several thin layers
covered by an orange nylon
jacket he'd been wearing for
the better part of a decade
tea toast two eggs two sausage
and a danish Leo was a thin man
but not necessarily a healthy
one exactly the type you'd
expect to see stopping in
early at a place like this on
his way to the bait shop on
a day like today

union wages

driving out of town in a navy blue 92
Chevy Corsica with a slight lean to the
driver side Ernest gently felt the front
pocket of his denim shirt containing
exactly 17 days of union wages and a receipt
for a full tank of gasoline the back seat
brimmed with what little was salvageable
from the apartment above Stanley Hardware
a bird cage full of dirty laundry portable
cd player with broken tape deck 2 pairs of steel
toe Wolverines 4 DeWalt boxes of miscellany
perhaps the only items not taken in his haste
were the family album and his lawyer's cell
number hoping to never again need either

accidents and bravado

mayflies night crawlers and the morning dew
it was this same time last May that we made
the trip to NH i woke with my left pinky and
ring finger gone numb after passing out with
my sleeping bag on a rock causing me
to drop the oar the tackle the sunscreen into
Bear Pond us rowing in circles as i cursed
down the sun aha! and you you laughed Scotty
you laughed at all my outrageous stories stories
about mini-golf accidents and batting
cage bravado the very sort you expect to
hear when drinking the night into the dawn

Chuck's favorite azalea

with a cherry stone lodged
in the rear of his throat Chuck
watched helpless as the potted
azalea tumbled over the porch
railing a shattering of plastic
as it met with the graying
asphalt below gasping for air and
otherwise lifeless Chuck estimated
the neighbor's Dachshund was already
devouring the remnants green
planting pot and all

as a child

sitting here tonight
thinking of a photograph of
you as a small child your
pigtails tied with red yarn to
match your corduroy overalls and
you're dying Easter eggs
in the kitchen or picking
dandelions out back or washing
the Ford with Grandpa Jack
in the driveway I don't know because
i've'nt yet seen this photograph
but it must exist Karin these things
litter closets all across America

small potatoes

pieces of asphalt have
broken apart from the
street out front becoming
embedded in Greg's lawn over
the course of the Winter some
as small as dimes others as
large as small potatoes
and weeds now new ones
every day and flowers too
the legacy of previous owners
purple blue yellow and it
all gets mowed over today
in the interest of time

the archeologist

the well out beyond the rock
wall returned muddled echoes in
the soft evening dusk it was older
than the town he'd been informed a
relic of the Meyer Farm he'd
dug up quite a bit of the
ground around the well and found
bits of bone rusted wheel spokes
and jars of what may have once been
preserves but now looked like
thick ancient vomit Tommy could only
imagine how many buckets of
water the well'd relinquished over
time or how many items had been
deposited into that dark dampness
by the curious he himself could only
account for a single Wookie and
two empty root beer cans

Spring cleaning

Carl wanted desperately to issue a warning to
broadcast a statement before
it was too late and it was too late
family and friends and old soccer buddies
clogged the courthouse hallways to offer
support and shout a few harsh vulgarities
Margaret went so far as to set up her
folding table normally assigned strictly
to bake sale duties and drafted a
petition on the spot only to find out
later that the misspelling of Carl's
middle name had stripped it of
any legitimacy it may have had
and all the while the proper authorities
with the proper paperwork transferred
the contents of Carl's split level ranch
into black plastic bags and white
file boxes enough evidence
to ensure the trial'd be a mere formality

the explorer

the stream ran perpendicular
to the back of the Ding's
property Billy knew this from
a math text he hadn't much
used this year his back pocket
brimming with popsicle sticks
painstakingly sharpened along
the asphalt sidewalk he
used a broken hockey stick
to make his way through the new
overgrowth overgrowth that Billy
hadn't anticipated when he buried
his treasure last Fall but there
it was 53 paces to the right of
the tree with a hole like a
urinal in the trunk buried a
foot deep in a fake antique
Oreo tin covered with a Ziploc
storage bag preserved through
the long Winter Billy's prized
possession stared back at him
4 naked ladies posing on
a dune buggy a single page
hastily removed from a Swank
magazine at the Frost Convenience
this site marked the spot that he'd
make camp at this Summer

no argument

Paul wore her mood ring
back then when they'd
spend the nights talking
until dawn tracing their
shadows on the wall with
tingling fingertips and
whispers slow and melodic
back then before it slipped
from his hand lost to the
log flume he operated at the
water park on the outskirts
of town near the drive-in
and the Rod & Gun club by
then Claire'd never expected
him to return it a form of
apathy that had become the
foundation of their relationship
that Summer by the lake
they'd drive into the mountains
and drive back from the mountains
with not a word between them
at night she'd film their sex
acts and never let him watch
filing the tape in a drawer to
be experienced later alone when
she'd get high and masturbate

recycling

Bert'd been using the vacant lot
as a staging area for his new
recycling and removal business
since his parole in early Spring
and not a soul had questioned
his presence on Sheldon Street acting
as if he owned the land Bert was
spending 7 days a week hauling in
used mattresses from the old folk
homes recycling bricks telephone
poles and tires reducing toilets
sinks tubs and tile to rubble he'd
placed an ad in the local
paper for part time help
knowing it was only a matter of
time before he was forced off
the lot Bert was determined
to make every cent he could be-
fore leaving the lot the mess
and the authorities behind

the Saturday market

markedly different in appearance
they arrive at the marketplace
a single row of fish pasta meat
pastry and vegetable stalls he
watches as Heather fingers a bushel
of carrots in an attempt to discern
freshness rigorous quick and calculated
no one would deny the expertise of
her scrutiny Tim'd never seen so
many haggard women women that
looked and smelled as though they
just sprouted from the earth
alongside their crop he feels
like a tourist in his sandals
and gabardine shorts his wallet
thick with white collar wages and
department store credit but his
spirits lift as Heather loads
his arms with paper wrapped
meats and blocks of cheese
with a sense of accomplishment
they walk home along the
waterfront her surefooted boots
making easy work of the cobble-
stone that trips Tim up

at East Hill Farm

we'd set out for Troy, NH every
Summer every 4th of July week
my father'd have The Dave Brubeck
Quartet Time Out cassette
queued up ready to play as soon
as we'd gone out of range of
the morning Celtic radio
program and there was
always Juicy Fruit in his car i'd
almost always get sick on
the final winding road
up past Gap Mountain but by
the time we'd reached the inn
and saw Mount Monadnock rising
from across the pond i'd be
off racing my brother to the
chicken coop in search of
fresh eggs or to the gift shop
for a bag of mixed candy
and bottled soda

mail-in

waiting on a rebate always a
rebate to the point that Bruce
is afraid to remodel the front
room or upgrade the pc or try
a new motor oil and always the
rebate arrives but the waiting
the tension oh man the waiting
is the real gut-punch left him
sleeping in the front shrubs
last Wednesday in sick anticipation
of a $14 Dust Buster mail-in spent
much of May tweezing his eyebrows
in the half bath in a nervous effort
to stay sharp only now sweat it
gets in Bruce's eyes hooked
on a paint mail-in now and yes
tossing back Pabst Blue Ribbon
from Sunday to Sunday and again
until Sunday and the rebates there
are always the rebates

the NA double-C

when Wednesday comes i'll
be coming to terms with
the overgrowth and with the
Neighborhood Auxiliary Care
Committee I'll be painting rusting
wrought iron fences I'll be replacing
damaged letter boxes you've your
burdens i've mine should i wait for a more
spectacular day should i wander about
St Thomas' gravestones for further
inspiration should i stop off at
Carver Pond to wrangle geese
should i sucker punch unsuspecting
Summer help over at Swan Cleaners
no i'll kneel at the heart of
Lake Nippenicket and stroke a bass
until night falls around us

Summer help

she'd applied for the part time
Summer help at the cleaners after
seeing the window advertisement while
leaving the liquor store Janet was
offered the position and was thankful
she'd worn the low cut blue sleeveless
top and not the modest ruffled blouse she
had originally tried on it was supposed
to be a simple way to pass the time
while Billy was away at camp and the
Professor was off on sabbatical in
the Welsh countryside but after just
8 shifts the chemicals in the air were
giving Janet headaches and possibly even
hives and on more than one occasion
she required intervention from Mr Swan
just in the nick of time as customers became
overbearingly belligerent when faced with a
multitude of missing bedspreads trousers
blazers and assorted draperies

at the last minute

a 'Dam Engineer' Scotty
use to like to call himself with
a sly grin in the years before
he took his unseen leap he
wipes his sweaty palms once
across the back pockets
of his pale dungarees not so
much nervous but hot and
tired the hazard lights of the
Olds Cutlass click rhythmically
off and on on the side of the
overpass the afternoon sun glares
off windshields of the afternoon
traffic flowing along the sweltering
highway below this is Scotty's
reckoning and Scotty's only

sitting vigil

could taste the old lady's
chowder as the cream
laden air crawled its
way along the bar i'd
lost count and was
quickly becoming famished
i'd enough left for a few
cheap drafts and a modest
amount of whiskey having
consumed these i clamored
to my feet and saluting no
one in particular spilled
out onto the dark side street
across from Brick's Washateria
the night air was thick and
heavy with three days of
continuous humidity and the
varied humming of air conditioners
and box fans as i stumbled my
way south on Hall Street and
home and now finishing off the
remnants of a Milwaukee's
Best 12 pack out on the back porch
i look out upon the vending
machine graveyard and wonder
if Scotty'll make the morning papers

middle

i've pitched a half dozen bottle
caps into the tall river grass just
out of view of the Mt Feake Cemetery
sound of bagpipes tumbles down the
hill just outside my reach settling
in the river current headed for the
Moody Street dam with the straight noon
sun hot on the top of my ears it seems
like just the right sort of day for
being alive still i'm reticent about
leaving this place not this riverbank
not this mortal realm but this town this
history mine and the town's i've been
packed for the better part of the week
well beyond the lease it would stand to
reason that there is certainly something
waiting for me on the other side of this
12 pack and still i wait for some sort
of sign on the faces of the joggers
running by

another working relationship

had felt I'd linger about
until at the very least late
Autumn but it had become abundantly
obvious to me that Bert entertained
ideas of ridding himself of my services
earlier it being clear in the way
he licked his lips each every
morning when he greeted me out
at the faded green tool shed over
on Sheldon's Vacant Lot that's why it
didn't come as any kind of surprise this
morning when after catching me
spitting in his coffee Bert walked me
out back to a shallow grave he'd
prepared and with a single swift solid
swing struck me with a spade in the
back of the skull now that I'm laying face
down in a shallow dusty hole on Sheldon's
Vacant Lot the morning sun
hot on my neck it has gotten to the
point where I now nearly regret poisoning
Bert's old Golden Retriever Gunther

Acknowledgements:

To those who helped with this book, both directly and indirectly, I'd like to give my thanks.

First and foremost I'd like to thank my wife and best friend Karin. As well as my family, Mom, Dad, and Mike, for always being there.

For assistance with the writing of this volume I'd like to thank Brian Tracy, Steve Harding and Derek Guivens for providing invaluable assistance and encouragement. I'd especially like to thank Chris Rubino for being the driving force behind this project and for acting as my sounding board for the last 20 years. Without his involvement this project would never have been completed.

About the Author:

D Edward Ennis is living a comfortable life with his wife and two pugs. He enjoys reading and napping during his lunch breaks. He has never injured himself by falling off his house while trying to paint it. He has never told a lie.

www.ingramcontent.com/pod-product-compliance
Ingram Content Group UK Ltd.
Pitfield, Milton Keynes, MK11 3LW, UK
UKHW020241250726
13967UKWH00001B/487